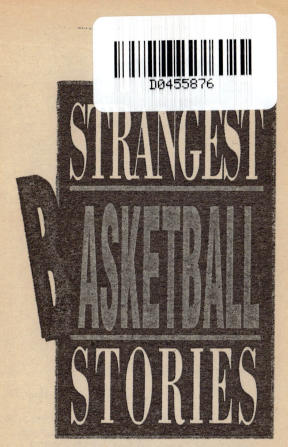

STRANGEST BASKETBALL STORIES

by Bart Rockwell

Watermill Press

Metric Equivalents

1 inch = 2.540 centimeters

1 foot = 0.305 meters

1 mile = 1.609 kilometers

Cover illustration by Paulette Bogan.

LIBRARY OF CONGRESS CATALOGING-IN-PUBLICATION DATA
Rockwell, Bart, (date)
    World's strangest basketball stories / by Bart Rockwell.
        p.   cm.
    Summary: Relates unusual stories and facts from the history of
basketball.
    ISBN 0-8167-2935-2 (lib. bdg.)   ISBN 0-8167-2852-6 (pbk.)
    1. Basketball—United States—Anecdotes—Juvenile literature.
[1. Basketball—Miscellanea.   2. Basketball—History.]   I. Title.
GV885.1.R63   1993
796.323'0973—dc20   92-25676

SMALL-FRY CENTER

To be a good center in basketball, a player has to be tall, right? Not necessarily! At least that wasn't the case in 1953 when a center named Johnny O'Brien of Seattle University was named to the Associated Press All-America team. O'Brien was only 5'9". Even if he didn't have the usual size of an all-American center, he certainly had the credentials. He averaged over 28 points per game in his junior and senior years and tallied over 2,500 points in his college career.

The story doesn't end here. Johnny had a twin brother who also played on the Seattle team. Eddie O'Brien was a 5'9" starting guard. After college, the O'Brien twins signed to play pro *baseball* with the Pittsburgh Pirates, and both played several years in the majors. Perhaps they didn't think they were tall enough to play in the National Basketball Association (NBA)!

PERFECT NAME

F ranconia College in New Hampshire had no
home court during the early 1980's. The team
played all of its games on the road. Nevertheless, the
team always felt right at home whenever its players
looked up at the other team's scoreboard. The
Franconia College basketball team was nicknamed
the Visitors.

NO QUICK RELEASES

n 1978 coach Don DeVoe of the University of
Tennessee was very impressed with Terry
Glenn, a walk-on player who tried out for the team.
DeVoe even thought enough of Glenn to offer him a
basketball scholarship. Unfortunately, the young
man couldn't accept the offer, because he'd never be
able to travel with the Tennessee team to out-of-state
games. At the time, Glenn was a prisoner at the
Knoxville work-release center, and was enrolled at
Tennessee with the permission of the State
Corrections Department.

FORGETFUL!

W hen Dick Garrison took off his warm-up sweat
pants and prepared to go into a game for Ohio
University in 1953, was he ever embarrassed.
Garrison had forgotten to put on his trunks and had
to run for the safety of the locker room!

FOLLOW THE BOUNCING BALL

Pete Maravich was one of the most exciting basketball players in the history of the game. When Pete was young, he loved basketball so much that he carried a basketball around with him almost everywhere he went. He used to dribble a ball while riding around on his bike, and he even took one along with him when he went to the movies. In the movie theater Pete always sat on the aisle so he could practice dribbling while watching the flick!

WHERE'S THE COACH?

The Los Angeles Lakers had trouble keeping a coach on the bench during the 1979 season. When head coach Jack McKinney was injured in a freak bicycle accident, Paul Westhead became the Lakers' interim coach while McKinney was recovering. But then Westhead had to temporarily give up his coaching duties to have a kidney stone removed. In stepped assistant coach Pat Riley, who became the Lakers' interim head coach. Coach Riley went on to become a highly successful NBA coach.

FIVE-YEAR PLAN

Five years is a long time to play basketball without winning a single game. Nevertheless, Carbondale (Pennsylvania) Sacred Heart's girls' basketball team did just that from December 22, 1981, until December 18, 1986.

Sacred Heart defeated Blue Ridge High School 47–46 in overtime on December 22, 1981, and then went almost five years without another victory. The team lost 141 straight games. Finally, on December 18, 1986, Sacred Heart beat Mountain View High School 41–38 to end its long losing streak.

LIKE FATHER, LIKE SON

Joey Meyer has been the head basketball coach at DePaul University for a number of years. Under Meyer, DePaul has enjoyed great success.

Prior to Joey's reign as head coach, DePaul had another coach with the last name of Meyer who guided the school to many basketball victories. That head coach's name was Ray Meyer, and he was Joey's dad. When Ray Meyer retired after some 40 years as a head coach, his son and assistant coach Joey Meyer took over his dad's job. Even in basketball, the old saying "like father, like son" holds true.

BASKETBALL LAW

Is it against the law for a referee to make bad calls during a high school basketball game? An Oklahoma officer seemed to think so in a game between Douglas High School and Spencer High School on February 6, 1992. When a star Spencer player was knocked down in the middle of a tense overtime period, a police officer stormed out of the stands and onto the court.

The police officer went up to the referee and warned him and the Douglas High coach about excessive physical play. When the referee protested that the basketball game was out of the lawman's jurisdiction, the officer pushed the referee off the court and threatened to arrest him! The ref was then escorted out of the gym, where other police officers and several basketball officials met with him. In the end, the ref didn't get arrested for not calling enough fouls, but Spencer High went on to win the game anyway, 44–43!

WHAT ARE YOU DOING HERE?

In college basketball, a player is allowed five personal fouls. After the fifth foul, the player is disqualified and has to spend the rest of the game on the sidelines. At least that's what the rule states. But it doesn't always happen that way. Take the case of Otis Smith, a guard who played for coach Bob Wenzel's Jacksonville University Dolphins in 1984.

Jacksonville was playing against the Old Dominion University Monarchs in a tight, hard-fought game. Otis Smith, a guard for the Dolphins, was playing very aggressively and picked up his fifth personal foul with 2 minutes, 44 seconds left to go in the game. Before the Old Dominion player who was fouled could shoot his free throws, a time-out was called.

During the time-out, the referee notified the scorer's table that Smith had fouled out of the game. The time-out ended and the teams retuned to the floor. Smith was supposed to sit down, but instead went back into the game—and nobody seemed to notice. Smith played a little over a minute and a half in a game he'd fouled out of before the mistake was noticed by the officials. Smith claimed that no one had informed him that he'd fouled out. Old Dominion shot and scored two technical fouls, but it didn't help. Jacksonville won the game 79–68!

TEMPER, TEMPER!

T he Rochester Zeniths played in the Continental Basketball Association in 1981. The CBA is the oldest pro league still in operation in the country (it was founded in 1946 as the Eastern League). The Continental Basketball Association may be long on tradition, but unfortunately it had some players with short tempers in 1981.

In a game between the Zeniths and the Montana Golden Nuggets, Norman Bounds, a Zeniths hometown favorite, finally got into the game. The crowd went wild as Bounds scored on a lay-up. But the official whistled the play dead and singled him out for a traveling infraction, which nullified his basket. Bounds went wild and chased after the official, who quickly hit him with two technical fouls and ordered him to leave the court. Bounds angrily headed off the floor. On his way to the dressing room he passed a water cooler. In a fit of temper, pushed the cooler out onto the court. He then kicked it, causing water to spill all over the floor. The fans loved his temperamental show, but the officials didn't. They sent Norman Bounds to the showers.

HEADS UP

Basketball coach Joe Lapchick was well known for his emotional outbursts during basketball games. Once while coaching the New York Knicks, Lapchick saw something happen in a game that upset him. He happened to be reaching for a cup of water from a tray filled with water cups, so he vented his anger by seizing the tray and hurling it into the air. Unfortunately for Lapchick, the tray, the cups, and the water all came back down right on top of his head!

BAD TIMING

Franklin and Marshall College was playing Colgate University in the Hofstra Basketball Tournament in December 1986 when a strange time-out cost Colgate the game.

With time running out, Colgate's coach, Joe Baker, reminded his players that they were out of time-outs. But when Franklin and Marshall scored to tie the game at 71–71 with only one second remaining, the Colgate players panicked. They immediately called for a time-out, forgetting what their coach had told them. Because Colgate was out of time-outs, the official called a technical foul on the team. As the Colgate players watched in disbelief, a Franklin and Marshall player stepped to the foul line and sank the game-winning foul shot with only a second to go. Since the foul was a technical, Franklin and Marshall also got the ball after the shot. They inbounded it and happily watched the game end. It was a strange defeat for Colgate, and it was all because of an untimely time-out.

SWEDISH SCORING MACHINE

In 1974 a boy in Sweden had a pretty good day in a basketball tournament. Thirteen-year-old Mats Wermelin led his teammates as they crushed their opponents by the unbelievable score of 272–0.

What makes the story even more amazing is that Wermelin is reported to have scored all of his team's 272 points!

FOUL EXPERIENCE

Even though basketball is supposed to be a noncontact sport, the game can get pretty rough sometimes. When one Kansas high school, Hillcrest, took on another, St. John's, in a girls' basketball contest on December 16, 1988, the game got very physical indeed. A total of 69 fouls were called! By the time there was only three minutes remaining in the game, three St. John's players had fouled out and five of the six players on the Hillcrest squad had also fouled out.

At that point the only player left on the court for Hillcrest was a sophomore guard who hadn't even suited up for the game because she was too sick to play. She was pressed into service when her teammates began to foul out, and she even had to wear a borrowed uniform.

Luckily for the sophomore, she didn't have to try to overcome St. John's 61–57 lead all by herself. Under Kansas State High School Activities Association rules, a basketball team must have at least two players in the game at all times. So the contest was called off with three minutes remaining, and St. John's was declared the winner.

SNACK ATTACK

The Utah Jazz basketball squad was getting walloped by the home-team Los Angeles Lakers in an NBA contest on March 12, 1985. It became evident to everyone that Utah had no chance of getting back into the contest. The score was 123–108 in the fourth period, and the Lakers were dominating play at both ends of the court. Things were so bad that fans started to leave the game.

Since Utah's head coach, Frank Layden, was feeling depressed about his team's performance and a bit hungry, he too decided to leave and go out for a snack. Layden turned control of the Utah team over to his assistant. He then left the basketball arena while the game was going on and went out to a nearby deli to grab a sandwich. The Jazz lost the game, but thanks to his snack coach Layden lost his ravenous appetite at the same time.

WAY TO GO

When basketball great Bill Russell left the University of San Francisco and joined the Boston Celtics, he made a wise move. In back-to-back seasons (1956–57) he went directly from a championship college basketball team to a championship pro basketball team, becoming the first player to do that.

PHYSICAL PLAY

When you play physical basketball, you sometimes commit personal fouls. John Carty of the
University of California Golden Bears played some
very physical basketball in his first college start, a
game against the University of Arizona in February
1988. In fact, he managed to pick up three quick
fouls in the first three minutes of the game. In most
college conferences, a player is allowed five personal
fouls before being disqualified, so Carty was quickly
removed from the game by his coach.

It wasn't until the start of the second half that
Carty returned to the court. As quick as a wink, he
picked up right where he left off. Carty notched two
more fouls in the opening two minutes of the second
half. Since he had used up all five of his personal
fouls, he was out of the game after playing a total of
just five minutes. Amazingly, John Carty had
managed to average one foul per minute in his first,
strange start as a college player.

TOURNAMENT TERRORS

Only one college has ever won both the National
Collegiate Athletic Association (NCAA)
basketball tournament and the National Invitation
Tournament (NIT) in the same year. It happened in
1950, and the unlikely champion of those two
tournaments was tiny City College of New York
(CCNY). Strangely enough, CCNY beat the same
team in both of those finals to take the crowns. CCNY
beat Bradley University 69–61 to win the NIT, and
defeated them again 71–68, to take the NCAA title.

THE HEARTBEAT OF BASKETBALL

Basketball is an exciting game, but it can also be stressful, especially for coaches. In a study done in 1979, a Brigham Young University professor found that the heart rates of head coaches during games average almost 100 percent above the average person's resting heart rate.

Unfortunately, coaches can't get rid of their stress by actually playing the game. They must relieve the stress another way. According to the BYU professor, one of the best ways coaches can do that is to yell a lot (even at the referee) and to pace up and down on the sidelines during a basketball contest.

WHAT'S THE SCORE?

T he coach of a losing basketball team can blame a lot of people. He can blame his players. He can blame the officials. He can even blame himself. But when Penn State played the University of Maryland in March 1990, losing Maryland coach Gary Williams could have blamed the scoreboard operator for the loss, and with good reason.

It happened in the second round of the National Invitation Tournament. With 34 seconds left in the contest, Maryland's Jerrod Mustaf hit what appeared to be a game-tying three-point jump shot. After the shot, the scoreboard showed the score, tied at 78–78, but the officials on the court ruled Mustaf's shot to be only a two-pointer. So contrary to what was shown on the scoreboard, Maryland trailed Penn State 78–77.

Unfortunately, it wasn't until there were only 16 seconds left in the game that the scoreboard operator finally corrected his mistake and put the right score on the board. And no one told the Maryland players, who didn't notice they were losing until only ten seconds of play remained. Frantically Maryland rushed to foul a Penn State player to stop the clock. Now there were only five seconds remaining in the game. Penn State's Freddie Barnes hit two free throws, and time ran out on Maryland. Penn Sate went on to win 80–77. Who was to blame for Maryland's loss? Just ask the scorekeeper.

AIR BALL

Pro basketball players are supposed to be good shooters, and a foul shot is supposed to be fairly easy to make. That's why some people call the foul line the charity stripe. But Garfield Smith, who played for the Boston Celtics in 1971, was a terrible foul shooter. That year Smith hit a measly 6 of 31 foul shots for a poor .194 average. One of his worst days at the line came in a game against the Phoenix Suns on November 17, 1971. Smith stepped to the line and was allowed to take three shots to score a maximum of two points. His first shot went to the left and missed everything—a classic air ball. His next shot was another air ball. His third and final shot likewise missed the rim, the net, and the backboard for air ball number three. Three consecutive air balls from an NBA player! You might not be surprised to learn that the 1971–72 season was Garfield Smith's last in the NBA.

SLIP SLIDING AWAY

B asketball games sometimes get called off for strange reasons. One of the strangest postponements ever involved a 1966 hoop contest between Dallas Baptist College and Tyler Junior College. The game was postponed because the court was just too slippery to play on! Apparently the floor had been repaired and then heavily waxed. The court was so slick that the players couldn't maneuver on it. So the game just slipped off the teams' schedules until it could be played at a later date.

TIME TO MAKE HER MOVE

W hen a team is in trouble, a star player really has to pitch in. The Hillsborough (New Jersey) High School Lady Raiders had scored only 11 points and were losing to conference rival Watchung Hills when Lady Raiders star player Sandi Everett decided it was time to make her move. Everett scored her team's last 20 points, including the game-winning bucket with 25 seconds remaining, to give Hillsborough a 31–30 victory over Watchung Hills on January 13, 1991.

HERE WE GO AGAIN

Gastonia is a small town in North Carolina. It's a place where two childhood friends, Eric Floyd and James Worthy, grew up playing basketball together. When they got older, they went to different high schools, Floyd to Hunter Huss High and Worthy to Gastonia Ashbrook High. When Floyd was a junior and Worthy was a sophomore, their two schools met in the finals of the state championship. Floyd's Hunter Huss High edged Worthy's Gastonia Ashbrook High by a single point to take the title.

After high school, Floyd and Worthy both went to college on basketball scholarships and became All-Americans. Floyd was an all-American at Georgetown, while Worthy was an all-American at the University of North Carolina.

In March 1982 Georgetown played North Carolina in the finals of the NCAA basketball tournament, and Floyd and Worthy faced each other in a championship game again. This time Worthy got his revenge for that one-point loss to Floyd in the high school championship game. Worthy's North Carolina team edged Floyd's Georgetown team for the title, 63–62. Again the difference was only one point. Both men went on to star in the NBA.

RAIN MAN

Jerry West was an outstanding college basketball player at West Virginia, where he won All-America honors. He was also a great NBA player and helped lead the Los Angeles Lakers to many winning seasons. West always loved playing basketball, even as a young boy. Once when he was ten years old, Jerry got in trouble with his parents for playing basketball outside in a driving rainstorm with one of his friends. It was raining so hard that Jerry had come into the house three times to change from soggy sneakers into dry ones.

CLOSE CALL

In a 1979 NBA game between the Golden State Warriors and the San Diego Clippers, a veteran NBA official suffered a heart attack while refereeing the game. Luckily, there were six cardiologists in the stands to help out the two team doctors, who rushed to the official's assistance. Fortunately, the official was well taken care of and rushed to a nearby San Diego hospital, where he recovered.

FAMILY AFFAIR

It's not easy playing on a basketball team that your older brother or sister played on before you. You sometimes have to live up to your older sibling's standards. But if you think that kind of situation is tough, consider the plight of point guard Mike North, who played for New Jersey's Dunellen High School in 1990. Mike, the youngest of nine children, found playing for his high school basketball team a real family affair. Dunellen's athletic director and the coach of the boys' varsity basketball team was someone named Jerry North, who just happened to be Mike's oldest brother!

RECORD GAME

On January 6, 1982, Cheryl Miller had a pretty good day for a high school basketball player. Cheryl set a modern high school girls' scoring record by hitting 46 of 50 field goals and 13 of 15 free throws for an amazing total of 105 points in a single game! Cheryl's record helped California's Riverside Poly High defeat Norte Vista High 179–15. Cheryl's record is a modern record because in the early days of girls' high school basketball, not all players were allowed to shoot, and each team had designated shooters. Today girls' basketball is played by the same rules that govern boys' games.

REFEREE HAZARD

In the second round of the 1992 National Invitation Tournament, Manhattan College took on the Rutgers University Scarlet Knights in a big college matchup. The game was a hard-fought contest, but it looked as if Rutgers would emerge the winner, as the Knights led 61–60 with 13 seconds remaining and also had possession of the ball out of bounds.

Rutgers' Creighton Drury did the inbounding honors. He saw the Knights' top scorer, Steve Worthy, break into the open and tossed him the ball. Worthy could have gone in for a breakaway lay-up but chose instead to run around and dribble away the seconds on the clock.

Unfortunately, one of the officials didn't see Worthy change direction and got in his way. Worthy and the official almost collided, and the ball bounced off the official and rolled free. Rutgers and Manhattan players dove for the ball, and it was ruled a held ball. The possession arrow favored the Manhattan Jaspers, and they got possession with seven seconds remaining. The Jaspers' Chris Williams took the inbound pass, dribbled the length of the court, and made a basket to give Manhattan a 62–61 lead with one second remaining. Manhattan went on to win the game, and Rutgers was eliminated from the 1992 NIT with a little help from a referee who was in the wrong place at the wrong time.

SHIRT TALE

Joe Lapchick was one of basketball's funniest and most colorful coaches in both the pro and the college ranks. Lapchick was directing the St. John's University (New York) Redmen during the 1961–62 season when his team went on a winning streak at the end of the year.

Lapchick was superstitious and didn't want to do anything to change his team's luck. He wore the same dirty shirt over and over again as his team won 11 straight games. Since he refused to wash the good luck out of the shirt, it soon got pretty smelly. Nevertheless, Lapchick continued to wear the shirt. He'd arrive for all of the St. John's basketball games in a clean shirt and then change into the dirty, lucky shirt when the game began. At the end of the season, Lapchick's wife tossed out the grimy shirt—good luck and all!

WHAT A DAY

One of the most appropriate college matchups to air on television in 1992 was a game played on February 17, President's Day. The game pitted George Washington University (named after America's first president) against James Madison University (named after America's fourth president).

LAST BUT NOT LEAST

The 1966 NBA All-Star Game was held at the home arena of the Cincinnati Royals (who are known today as the Sacramento Kings). Since the game was to be played in Cincinnati, Adrian "Odie" Smith, a Royals player, was a late addition to the All-Star roster. Smith wasn't really a great player. He was put on the team just to please the hometown fans. But when game time rolled around, Smith showed everyone he truly deserved to be a member of the NBA East All-Stars. Smith pumped in 24 points to lead his East squad in scoring. Amazingly, the player who was a late addition to the roster just to please the crowd ended up being voted the Most Valuable Player of the 1966 All-Star contest.

BIG FEET

The player who replaced Bob Lanier of the Detroit Pistons had to fill some pretty big shoes. Lanier wore size 22 sneakers!

GET THE POINTS

In 1963, West End High School of Alabama played Glenn Vocational High School and won the game 97–54. Walter Garrett had a big night for West End. He scored all of his team's 97 points!

NOT CAMERA SHY

On February 13, 1954, Furman University traveled to Newberry College to play a basketball game. The game was the very first sports event in the state of South Carolina to ever be televised live.

The game turned out to be a history-making broadcast for another reason, too. Playing for Furman was Frank Selvy, a great scorer who had been averaging close to 40 points a game that season. The cameras seemed to bring out the best in Frank. When the first half ended, he'd already tallied 37 points. When he added 25 more points in the third period (college games were played in quarters then) to up his game total to 62 points, fans everywhere realized something special was happening. With an entire quarter still to play, Selvy had a chance to break the major-college single-game scoring record of 73 points set by Bill Mlkvy of Temple. Selvy easily went on to pass Mlkvy's record and had a chance to notch 100 points a single game as time ticked down. With two seconds left to play, Selvy had 98 points as Furman inbounded the ball. They passed it to Selvy, who tossed up a desperation shot from just inside mid-court as the buzzer sounded. Amazingly, it went in! Frank Selvy set an NCAA Division I scoring record of 100 points in a single game.

HOW MANY POINTS?

Three-point plays are not rare in basketball games, but have you ever heard of an 11-point play? Don't say there is no such thing, because one occurred in 1979 and it helped Daniel Murphy High School of Los Angeles win a game it should have lost.

Notre Dame High School had just beaten Daniel Murphy High 67–61 in a hoop contest in California. The Murphy players had already left the floor when the Notre Dame coach went up to the game officials to complain about the job they'd done. The angered officials called technical fouls on the coach and his assistants. After three technicals, the Notre Dame coach was supposed to leave the floor, but he refused. Because of his refusal, and because the game had officially ended, the officials were allowed to assess him with an unlimited number of flagrant fouls. They ended up assessing him with 12.

Finally a player from the Daniel Murphy squad was called back on to the floor and given the opportunity to shoot 12 technicals in a game that was already over. Of the 12 shots, the player made 11, which gave Daniel Murphy a strange 72–67 win over Notre Dame. Sometimes a game isn't even over when it's over!

COAT OF ARMS

John Weinert was the head basketball coach at Bowling Green State University in 1981 Weinert had an odd, superstitious habit that year. He began every game without wearing the sport jacket he had brought to the contest. Only when he was absolutely positive that his team would win the game did Weinert dare put his jacket on.

CAN YOU BELIEVE IT?

In 1927 Drain High School and Wilber High School in Oregon got together for a game. The result was the lowest-scoring basketball game in high school history, as Drain won the contest 1–0.

Odd as that record is, it was duplicated by two high school teams in Illinois in March 1930. In an Illinois district tournament contest, Georgetown High School beat Homer High School by the same wacky score of 1–0!

NO SMALL FEAT

What does it take to make up a high school championship basketball team? Most people would say that it takes a lot of good players. After all, the more players a coach has to choose from, the better his chances are of putting together a winning combination. Then again, winning a championship might just be a matter of having the right nine players on the team.

Take the case of Beal Island High School in Maine. In 1950–51 the Beal Island High School boys' team won 24 games and lost only 1 on their way to capturing Maine's small-school state title. What's amazing about that feat is that Beal Island High School is actually a very small school on an island in the Atlantic Ocean. In 1950–51 Beal Island High had a total of only 11 boys in the entire school! Of those 11 boys, 9 played on the school basketball team and 1 more was the team manager. The only game Beal Island lost that year was a 38–37 defeat at the hands of a team it had clobbered 91–46 earlier in the season. So who says that when picking a winning team, the more players the merrier?

JINXED

Calvin Murphy of the Houston Rockets set an NBA record by making 78 consecutive free throws in a season from December 27, 1980, to February 28, 1981. In 1991 it began to look as if Ricky Pierce of the Seattle Supersonics might just beat Calvin's mark. Pierce went into the Supersonics game against the Boston Celtics in Boston with 75 consecutive free throws under his belt. But unfortunately for Pierce, he had bad luck. He missed his very first free throw attempt of the night to end his bid for a record. Pierce's streak came to a skidding halt on an appropriate date. The streak ended on Friday the 13th!

ONE-MAN TEAM

St. Peter's High School of Fairmont, West Virginia, had an intrasquad basketball game on March 16, 1937, that matched a team of seniors against a team of sophomores. During the game, all of the senior players fouled out except one: senior Pat McGee, who was left to defend against the sophomore team alone with the score tied 32–32 and only seconds to go in the contest. But McGee didn't do so badly for a one-man team. He held the sophs scoreless and netted three points to give his team a 35–32 victory!

FILL IT UP!

Talk about a hot hand. Using two basketballs and with the help of two rebounders, Ted St. Martin made 230 free throws in only ten minutes during a basketball shooting demonstration at Park Mall in Tucson, Arizona, on July 28, 1979. On June 25, 1977, he scored 2,036 *consecutive* free throws! St. Martin is a world-famous shooter who holds many similar basketball-shooting records.

ONE-ON-ONE

In 1965 Don Nelson was put on waivers after playing two seasons for the Los Angeles Lakers. He thought his NBA career might be over. Luckily for Nelson, Red Auerbach, the coach of the Boston Celtics, called and offered him a tryout. To make the team, Nelson would have to impress Auerbach by playing one-on-one against Ronnie Watts, a player already on the Celtics squad.

Nelson went to the tryout and played Watts one-on-one while Red Auerbach watched. Shortly after the tryout, Nelson was signed to a contract and joined the Celtics. And whom did Nelson replace on the Boston roster? Ronnie Watts!

TRY AGAIN

One of the best NBA players to ever handle a basketball was also one of the worst foul shooters in history. The great Wilt Chamberlain, who scored 31,419 points as an NBA star, was a rotten free-throw shooter. In fact, he missed more free throws than any other player in NBA history! Chamberlain attempted 11,862 free throws during his regular-season career (1960–73) and missed 5,805 of them. During the 1967–68 season, he missed 528 of 932 free throws. Chamberlain's lifetime *field-goal* percentage of .540 is higher than his lifetime *foul-shooting* percentage, which is .511. Now *that* is a strange stat!

STRANGE HABIT

Don Haskins, the head basketball coach at the University of Texas at El Paso, has an odd way of dealing with stressful game situations. The coach who led his El Paso team to the NCAA tourney in 1992 often refuses to watch games in close situations! He simply turns away from the action on the court or shields his eyes with his hands.

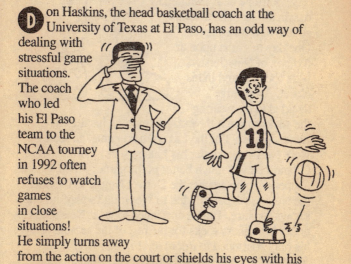

SOCK IT TO ME

Orlando Woolridge played for the Los Angeles Lakers in 1989. Before joining the Lakers, Woolridge had played for the Chicago Bulls and the New Jersey Nets, where he'd enjoyed some of his finest moments as a player. As a Nets player, he averaged over 20 points per game. Unfortunately, his game fell off just a bit when he first came to Los Angeles.

Woolridge badly wanted to regain the form he'd demonstrated as a Nets player. One day he came upon an old box of New Jersey Nets socks stored in his closet. Woolridge decided to try wearing the socks to see if they might improve his luck as a Lakers player. For the Lakers' next game, he secretly wore Nets socks under his Lakers socks. Amazingly, Orlando played much better in the game, which happened to be against the Denver Nuggets. Whether the Nets socks contributed to Woolridge's play, no one knows for sure. But he continued to wear Nets socks under his Lakers socks for the rest of the season, and his play continued to improve. In fact, Woolridge finished the 1989 season in fine form. Was it because of his socks? You'd have to ask Orlando Woolridge!

BENCH HELP

The 14–0 Temple University Owls were looking to remain undefeated when they played the University of Nevada at Las Vegas Runnin' Rebels on July 24, 1988. However, the Runnin' Rebels were 16–1 and looking to improve their record. They did, with a little help from their bench.

With less than a minute to go in the contest, UNLV was losing 58–54. Temple had the ball and was dribbling it upcourt. A UNLV player knocked the ball away. It looked as if the ball were going to bounce out of bounds near the Runnin' Rebels' bench. But suddenly, UNLV reserve player Richard Robinson got up off the bench and tapped the ball back to one of his teammates on the court. He then quickly sat down. Unbelievably, the officials did not see Richards give his side an illegal helping hand and allowed play to continue. The Runnin' Rebs got the ball and quickly made a three-point basket to shave Temple's lead to 58–57. Temple players protested, but to no avail. The officials simply didn't see Robinson's sneaky move. The basket counted, and UNLV went on to beat the frustrated Temple Owls 59–58.

BIG JUMP

Bill Willoughby made a big jump from high school basketball to the NBA in 1975. Willoughby, who graduated from a high school in New Jersey, was signed by the Atlanta Hawks without ever having played college basketball. He made his debut in the NBA for the Hawks on October 23, 1975, when he was only 18 years, 156 days old. Willoughby was the youngest man ever to play in the NBA. Although he never became a star, he played nine years in the NBA.

REALLY FOUL SHOOTING

Center Chris Dudley refused to accept charity during a game played between his New Jersey Nets and the visiting Indiana Pacers on April 14, 1990. In the fourth period of that contest, Dudley went to the charity stripe 13 times without making a single point. Dudley's 0-for-13 performance from the foul line was the worst free-throw demonstration in the history of the NBA. Even the great Wilt Chamberlain, who was a notoriously bad foul shooter, never did as poorly. Wilt once missed 10 free throws in a row, but no NBA player had ever missed 13 straight foul shots until Dudley's less-than-deadly performance in 1990.

OLYMPIC POWER

In 1936 basketball became part of the Olympic games. The United States Olympic basketball team won all seven Olympic basketball titles from 1936 to 1968, and they never lost a single contest. The U.S. string of 63 consecutive victories was finally broken when they lost to the Soviet Union 51–50 in the 1972 Olympic Games in Munich, West Germany.

SMASHING PERFORMANCE

P laying in his first college game at home in front of his family turned out to be a smashing debut for young Spencer Haywood in November 1968. Haywood, a forward for the University of Detroit Titans, not only brought down the house with his playing but also one of the glass back boards. Spencer helped crush Aquinas College in the game by piling up 36 points and pulling down 31 rebounds, as the Titans built up a 65-point lead over their helpless foe.

Late in the game Haywood went in for a slam dunk. But when he rammed the ball through the hoop, he also shattered the backboard into hundreds of pieces. Because there was no spare backboard on hand, a replacement was out of the question. The game couldn't continue. The officials decided that since Detroit was out in front of Aquinas 105–40 with just over six minutes left, they would call the game off then and there and credit Detroit with the win. No one argued the call, and everyone went home.

NOT A LOSER

Most basketball coaches have to win games to keep their jobs. That wasn't the case with Coach Herman "Red" Klotz. Klotz kept a coaching job with the same team for over twenty years even though his team lost over *7,500 games!*

Red Klotz was the playing coach of the Washington Generals, the team that travels around the globe with the Harlem Globetrotters. The Generals match up with the Globetrotters for most of their games. It isn't the Generals' job to lose (and they have won a game or two against the Globetrotters on rare occasions), but the Globetrotters almost always come away victorious. Of course Red didn't mind. Thanks to his team's peculiar role, his job was never on the line.

RAPID FIRE

Talk about quick scoring! In a game against Albright College (Pennsylvania), St. Thomas Aquinas College (New York) scored 4 field goals in a span of only 16 seconds. Unfortunately, St. Thomas Aquinas ended up losing the game!

UPSET PLAYERS

The players from Towns County High School of Clayton, Georgia, had gotten so frustrated and upset at the officials during a game that they decided to protest in a very strange way. They began shooting at their *opponent's* basket, and ended up scoring 56 points for the other team! Towns County High lost the game, 129–41.

PAPER DELIVERY

entral Michigan University fans had a strange way of showing their appreciation for their college basketball team. The Chippewas were showered with toilet paper thrown from the stands by fans during home games from 1986 to 1988.

The wacky practice started in early 1986 when angry fans showed their displeasure with the Chippewas' losing record by tossing a few rolls of toilet tissue out onto the court. However, as Central Michigan's team and record improved, the tissue tossing became a way of demonstrating fan appreciation. The practice became so popular that at times the entire court was covered with rolls of tissue. Sometimes games had to be halted for as long as five minutes so the mess could be cleared from the court. It became such a problem that for the 1988 season conference officials passed a special anti-toilet-tissue regulation that made it a technical foul for fans to throw toilet paper out on the court during a game. The new regulation soon ended the toilet-paper storms. You might say the practice went right down the drain.

BIG CHANCE

In 1979–80 the Detroit Pistons finished the NBA season with a rotten 16–66 record. To try to improve their team, the Pistons' management decided to hold an open house of sorts, in hopes of discovering a new superstar. Detroit general manager Jack McClosky announced that the team would have an open tryout for people who thought they could play pro basketball. The tryout was a week-long test held at Oakland University in suburban Detroit.

To Jack McClosky's surprise, over 390 players of all ages, shapes, and sizes showed up for the open-door tryout. More than 50 players six feet tall or shorter tried out. Over 100 came with only high school basketball experience under their belts. Some 30 players showed up for the tryout who had never even played basketball in high school! After it was all over, not a single player from the tryout camp ended up making the Pistons' roster for the next season. It just goes to show that a lot of people believe they could play in the NBA if given a chance, but they really couldn't. The Detroit Pistons' wacky tryout camp in 1980 certainly proved that.

BIG GUY

The tallest basketball player to ever be officially measured was Suleiman Ali Nashnush. He played for the Libyan national team in 1962 and was eight feet tall.

WHO?

The Northeastern University Huskies didn't get much respect in 1982. That year, in the NCAA tournament, the Huskies played St. Joseph's University (Pennsylvania) in the opening round.

When the public-address announcer introduced the Huskies squad, he said, "And now the starting lineup for Northwestern!" Getting their name mixed up in the introductions, however, didn't prevent Northeastern from upsetting St. Joseph's 63–62.

Unfortunately, the Huskies still got no respect in the *second* round of the tournament. When they arrived at their locker room to get ready for the game, the sign on the door read "Northeasten" instead of "Northeastern." Worst of all, the Huskies received no respect from Villanova, their opponent in the second round. Villanova beat Northeastern 76–72 in triple overtime.

BARBECUED TO THE BENCH

C ollege basketball players sometimes get benched for the strangest reasons. Take the case of Charles Davis and Jimmy Gray, who were regulars on the Vanderbilt University squad. In February 1981, Davis, Gray, and their teammates were in a hotel in Knoxville, Tennessee, waiting to play a game against the University of Tennessee. About an hour before the team meal, Davis and Gray felt hungry and couldn't wait to eat. The two Vanderbilt players called room service and ordered $17.00 worth of barbecued ribs to be sent to their room. Since Vanderbilt had a rule about its players not using room service, Coach Richard Schmidt got mad and benched his two starters. But here's the real rib. Without Davis and Gray in the game, Tennessee barbecued Vanderbilt on the court 77–72!

NOT SO SHORT

I n 1981 the Golden State Warriors chose a player in the eighth round of the NBA draft who was just a fraction of an inch shorter than the height of the world high-jump record at the time. The Warriors picked 7'8" Yasutaka Okayama, who was from Japan. Unfortunately, he had played only junior varsity basketball at Portland State (Oregon) University, and wasn't interested in signing an NBA contract. He decided to return to Japan, where his nickname is Chibi, which means "Shorty."

ZERO OUTPUT

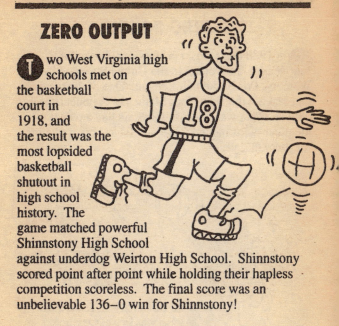

Two West Virginia high schools met on the basketball court in 1918, and the result was the most lopsided basketball shutout in high school history. The game matched powerful Shinnstony High School against underdog Weirton High School. Shinnstony scored point after point while holding their hapless competition scoreless. The final score was an unbelievable 136–0 win for Shinnstony!

BIG START

It's always nice if you can get your college coaching career off to a good start. And that is exactly what first-year coach Bill Hodges of Indiana State did in 1979. Hodges is the only rookie coach to ever take a team to the Final Four with a perfect record in his very first season. Hodges' Indiana State squad was 32–0 when it reached the NCAA finals in 1979. Indiana State ended up losing in the tournament to Michigan State 75–64, but no other head coach of a four-year school has ever gone to the Final Four with an unblemished record in his rookie season.

SEEING DOUBLE

In 1980 there was a professional basketball league for women in the United States called the Women's Pro Basketball League. One of the teams in that league, the New York Stars, had opponents seeing double. That was because the Stars had a pair of identical twins named Kaye and Faye Young playing for them that year!

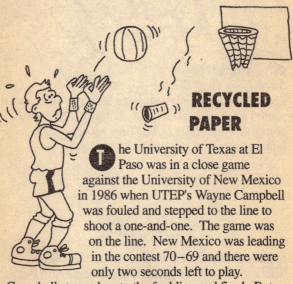

RECYCLED PAPER

The University of Texas at El Paso was in a close game against the University of New Mexico in 1986 when UTEP's Wayne Campbell was fouled and stepped to the line to shoot a one-and-one. The game was on the line. New Mexico was leading in the contest 70–69 and there were only two seconds left to play.

Campbell stepped up to the foul line and fired. But just as he did, a fan threw a paper cup at him from the stands—*after* he had released the ball. Campbell missed the bonus shot, and the game appeared to be over. But the official ruled that the thrown cup had distracted the UTEP shooter. The official voided the shot, which meant that Campbell got another chance to shoot. This time he made both foul shots, and UTEP beat New Mexico 71–70.

DON'T CHICKEN OUT

Basketball is a game that has a lot of fouls. But when little Trinity College played Yale University in 1954, the gym was filled with "fowls" of a different kind. The game was held on the Yale Bulldogs' home court. Fans of the Trinity College Bantams showed up in large numbers for the contest. Bantams are very small fighting roosters, and the Trinity College fans came prepared to flaunt their mascot. How it happened no one knows for sure, but Trinity College fans managed to smuggle dozens of live chickens into the Yale gym. After the Bantams scored their first basket, the fans tossed the chickens out onto the court! The chickens raced around the floor for several minutes and the game had to be delayed. When the chickens were finally collected, the game continued. The stunt was a great show of support for Trinity, but it was to no avail. Yale won the game 75–66.

THEY COULD HAVE PLAYED ALL NIGHT

When Kerrville Tivy High School played South San West High School in a game in Texas on January 5, 1980, it turned into a drawn-out affair. It took an astounding 10 three-minute overtimes to determine the final outcome of the contest!

When the buzzer sounded ending regulation play, the score was deadlocked at 43–43. Neither team scored in the first, second, or third overtime periods. In the fourth overtime, South San West hit a field goal with 30 seconds remaining, but Kerrville Tivy tied the score again on a buzzer shot. Both teams scored twice in the fifth overtime to knot the game at 49–49. The sixth, seventh, eighth, and ninth overtimes went scoreless. Finally Kerrville Tivy scored six points to South San West's two points in the tenth overtime to win the marathon game 55–51

RIPPED APART

In 1988 coach Scott Thompson of Rice University found his team in a heated contest against Texas A&M. During the game, Thompson got so angry during a time-out that he threw down his clipboard to emphasize a point. But after that brief display of temper, Coach Thompson quickly cooled down. Maybe it was because he felt a draft from behind. Throwing down the clipboard so angrily had caused the seam of his pants to split open in the back!

BORING BASKETBALL

W hen Oregon State University played Stanford University in a Pacific-10 contest in 1980, the meeting turned into one big, boring event. Stanford entered the game with a record of only 3–14, while OSU had won 19 games and lost only one. Stanford coach Dick DiBiaso figured the only chance his club had to beat Oregon was to slow down the game and stall. And stall is just what they did. The Stanford players took as much time as they could holding the ball and shot only when absolutely necessary. With less than ten minutes remaining in the game—and with the score tied at only 16–16—OSU scored on a lay-up to go out in front 18–16. Since they were now leading, Oregon borrowed Stanford's game plan, and *they* began to stall. Neither team scored again in the contest. When the final buzzer sounded, Oregon State had won its 20th game of the year by the boring score of 18–16 over Stanford.

SCARY STUFF

P hil Smith was a tough rookie guard for the NBA's Golden State Warriors in 1975. Smith never let the pressure of a big game affect him. He was always cool and calm during the season. But as soon as the season ended, Phil Smith got a bit rattled. As he was about to wed his college sweetheart in a big ceremony at the conclusion of the NBA season, cool-and-calm Phil Smith fainted at the altar before he could even say, "I do"!

FORGETFUL

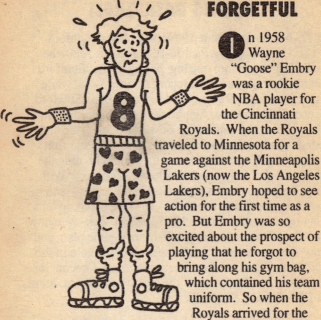

In 1958 Wayne "Goose" Embry was a rookie NBA player for the Cincinnati Royals. When the Royals traveled to Minnesota for a game against the Minneapolis Lakers (now the Los Angeles Lakers), Embry hoped to see action for the first time as a pro. But Embry was so excited about the prospect of playing that he forgot to bring along his gym bag, which contained his team uniform. So when the Royals arrived for the game, Embry didn't have a uniform to wear. Luckily, he managed to play anyway. He wore a borrowed Lakers' uniform turned inside out.

TALE OF THE TAPE

Carole Baumgarten, the head coach of the Drake University women's basketball team, had an upsetting habit during basketball games. Coach Baumgarten used adhesive tape like chewing gum. She would tear off a piece of tape during play and chew on it as if it were bubble gum! Sometimes, during the course of a single game, she would chew up an entire roll of tape. Now that's enough to give anyone an upset stomach!

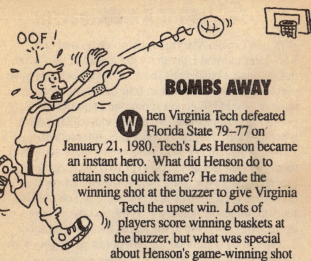

OOF!

BOMBS AWAY

When Virginia Tech defeated Florida State 79–77 on January 21, 1980, Tech's Les Henson became an instant hero. What did Henson do to attain such quick fame? He made the winning shot at the buzzer to give Virginia Tech the upset win. Lots of players score winning baskets at the buzzer, but what was special about Henson's game-winning shot was how far it traveled.

After a Florida State miss at the Tech basket, Henson pulled down the rebound. With time ticking away, he whirled and fired a perfect strike all the way down the court. At first it was thought the shot had traveled some 93 feet. But when the actual distance was measured, Les Henson's basket was found to have traveled an amazing 89 feet, 3 inches!

As incredible as that shot was, it's not the world's longest. Also at the buzzer, 17-year-old Christopher Eddy hit a shot that measured 90 feet, $2\frac{1}{4}$ inches to help his team, Fairview High School, defeat Iroquois High School 51–50 at Erie, Pennsylvania, on February 25, 1989. Eddy's shot is the current world record.

WHAT A PAIR

When Loyola Marymount University and U.S. International University get together, they often put on quite a basketball show. The two schools have played against each other in four of the top-scoring college basketball games (combined number of points) in history. The two teams scored *331* points when Loyola Marymount beat U.S. International 181–150 on January 31, 1989. When these same two teams met on January 5, 1991, LMU once again emerged the victor, 186–140, as the two teams combined for a total of 326 points. They combined for 306 points on January 7, 1989, as Loyola won again, 162–144. When the teams met on December 7, 1989, they combined for 289 points as Loyola won 152–137

Even though U.S. International wasn't involved in two other all-time high-scoring games, Loyola Marymount was. On November 28, 1988, Loyola Marymount beat Azusa Pacific University 164–138 for a two-team total of 302 points. On February 3, 1990, Louisiana State scored 148 points to Loyola Marymount's 141 points for a total of 289 points in one game. Now that's a lot of scoring!

GREAT RALLY!

In 1972 the Milwaukee Bucks were beating the New York Knicks 86–68 with only six minutes left to play. Incredibly, the Knicks rallied to score *the last 19 points* in the game to win 87–86!

DOUBLE BAD LUCK

Talk about rotten luck! On March 24, 1979, the New Jersey Nets lost not one but two games to the same team! Here's how it happened. The Nets traveled to Philadelphia to take on the 76ers in a regular-season contest. But before that game could begin, the teams had to replay the last 17 minutes of a game that had been suspended because of a protest earlier in the year. Because of the protest, the game could not count officially until those 17 minutes were replayed.

In the replay of the protested game, Philadelphia beat New Jersey 123–117 (the 76ers had also won the original game) for win number one of the night.

After an hour's rest, the teams took the floor again, and the 76ers defeated the Nets in the regularly scheduled game 110–98. Philadelphia officially won two games on the same night.

PASSED OUT

Every basketball coach knows that one key to winning games is passing the ball well. But sometimes you can have too much of a good thing. The University of Wyoming Cowboys once made 51 passes before taking a shot in a game they won against Brigham Young University by the score of 27–25. However, Wyoming's passing performance pales when compared with what Notre Dame once did in a 34–28 overtime loss to the University of Kentucky. In that game Notre Dame made 213 passes before taking a shot!

PIE GUYS

In 1980 the New York Knicks traveled west for a game against the San Diego Clippers. When the teams returned to the court after halftime, they discovered that the start of the second half would be delayed for a while. In fact it was delayed more than an hour. During halftime, there had been a pie-throwing contest, and pies had spilled all over the court. The players had to stand around and wait while the pies were cleaned off the court.

CHARITY GAME

Jamaica High School of Iowa once made 25 foul shots in a game against Bayard High School. And all of those points came in handy. Jamaica won its game against Bayard High by a score of only 25–16!

SORRY, HONEY

When the University of Utah defeated archrival Brigham Young University to take over first place in their conference, Utah coach Jack Gardner got excited. He was so excited that he could hardly think straight. He congratulated his players and then jumped in his car to drive home and celebrate. Unfortunately, Coach Gardner forgot something fairly impoitant. He had left his wife waiting for him in front of the gym! Luckily, he remembered his mistake halfway home and turned around to pick up his spouse.

PUBLICITY STUNT

A ndy Furman was in charge of the sports information department for Oral Roberts University in 1978. Furman cooked up several unusual publicity stunts to attract fans to the university's basketball games. When Oral Roberts squad played the Bulgarian national team that year, Furman arranged for anyone of Bulgarian ancestry to be admitted free to the game. Later that season, when a basketball squad from Hardin-Simmons University came to play Oral Roberts, he saw to it that any fans with the last name of Hardin or Simmons got in to the game free of charge!

IT DIDN'T MEASURE UP

W hen the Rutgers University Scarlet Knights traveled to Philadelphia for an Atlantic-10 clash against the St. Joseph's University Hawks, the start of the game had to be delayed 30 minutes. One of the basketball rims was found to be 9 feet 11 inches high instead of the regulation 10 feet high. The teams waited around as the rim was raised to the proper height.

WINNING IS EVERYTHING

S ome people claim that losing builds character. In the mid-1920's, the Passaic (New Jersey) High School basketball team didn't build character by losing, but it earned fame for winning. Passaic High won 159 basketball games in a row during those years. The massive winning streak was finally snapped when Passaic lost to Hackensack High School 39–35 in 1927.

DOG GONE!

When Bill Fouts officiated at a game between the University of Idado and Gonzaga University, he almost bit off more than he could chew. Gonzaga's mascot was a dog named Salty. And Salty, along with the Gonzaga fans and players, quickly became unhappy with Fouts' calls. The fans booed. The players complained. And Salty waited for just the right moment to register his displeasure.

The right moment for Salty turned out to be the wrong moment for Fouts. As the official stood near the Gonzaga bench, the angry dog snapped his leash. Salty raced over and bit Fouts on the leg.

Salty was tied up again, and Fouts' wound was treated. But the Gonzaga mascot's bite wasn't worse than the official's barking of fouls. Idaho ended up beating Gonzaga!

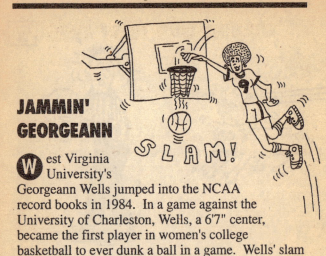

JAMMIN' GEORGEANN

West Virginia University's Georgeann Wells jumped into the NCAA record books in 1984. In a game against the University of Charleston, Wells, a 6'7" center, became the first player in women's college basketball to ever dunk a ball in a game. Wells' slam helped West Virginia to a 110–82 victory.

HE CAN'T LOSE

Bill Walton was a great NBA player who knew how to win games. Any team that had Bill Walton playing on it was hard to beat. When Bill was a student at Helix High School in San Diego, California, he led his team to a 49-game winning streak during his junior and senior years. Walton then went to UCLA, where he played on a freshman basketball team that went 20–0. As a college sophomore, he contributed to the astounding 88-game winning streak that UCLA had begun with 18 straight wins when Walton was playing on the freshman squad. Walton helped the varsity team win 70 games in a row before they finally lost to Notre Dame to snap the streak. In all, Bill Walton played 139 high school varsity, college freshman, and college varsity games without experiencing a single defeat!

WINNING ISN'T EVERYTHING

Setting an NCAA basketball record is usually something to be proud of. The Newark (New Jersey) branch of Rutgers University set an NCAA record in 1985, but they didn't feel very good about it. The record was for losing 47 straight basketball games! However, things looked up just one day after they set that depressing record. Rutgers–Newark won their very next game to end the two-year losing streak.

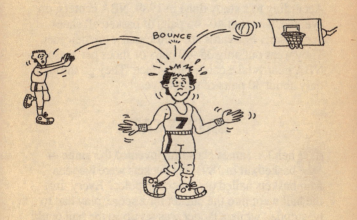

HEADY PLAYER

Larry Nelson of St. Cloud's Tech High School in Minnesota really used his head on the basketball court. In 1955 a teammate zipped Larry the ball when he wasn't looking. The basketball beaned Larry on the head, bounced up, and swished through the hoop, scoring two points for the St. Cloud team.

FOOT FEATS

Where would any basketball player be without basketball shoes? Basketball shoes suffer a lot of wear and tear, especially in the NBA.

According to a study done in 1989, NBA centers, on average, wear out 40–45 pairs of basketball shoes per season. Forwards are a little easier on their feet. They wear out only 35–40 pairs of shoes per season. NBA guards take care of their feet. They go through only about 30 pairs of shoes a year!

BASKET CASE

When Dr. James Naismith invented the game of basketball in 1891, his buckets were wooden fruit baskets nailed onto wooden poles. Every time the ball went into the bucket for a score, play had to be stopped while a ladder was set up so the ball could be retrieved from the basket.

As the sport grew in popularity, the fruit baskets were replaced by metal baskets with small holes in the bottoms. When a basket was made, play was then stopped while a long pole was inserted in the basket's hole to push the trapped ball up and out.

Finally, in 1913, basketball hoops with open bottoms that allowed the ball to drop through after a score were invented. These hoops made the game of basketball a lot easier.

NAME GAME

Varsity basketball coach Larry Murphy of Allagash High School in Maine had a strange name problem with his team players in 1978. Coach Murphy had to be on a first-name basis with all of his players to avoid confusion while making substitutions or shouting instructions. The problem was that of the 13 players on Coach Larry Murphy's squad, 6 had the last name Kelly and 3 had the last name McBreairty. And some people think Smith and Jones are common last names!

YIKES!

When it comes to games, you can't win them all, but it's encouraging to win one once in a while. Unfortunately, once in a while meant one win in over five years for the North Fulton High School (Georgia) girls' basketball team. North Fulton did not win a game from November 28, 1978, until December 5, 1983. The girls' team suffered through 107 consecutive losses before the squad finally beat Brown High School 36–30 in December 1983.

GOOD OLD DAYS

Jerry West was an All-Star player for the Los Angeles Lakers, and Kareem Abdul-Jabbar was a star performer for several NBA teams, including the Lakers. Not surprisingly, both were outstanding high school players too. When West played at Middletown High School in Ohio in the 1950's, he led his school to 76 straight wins. When Kareem Abdul-Jabbar (then known as Lew Alcindor) was a high school player for Power Memorial High in New York City, he led his team to 71 straight wins.

SWEAT SOCKS

Forward Kelly Tripucka, who played for several NBA teams, was a hard-working player who sweated a lot on the court. In fact, Tripucka once wore out *60 pairs* of basketball shoes in a single season! He perspired

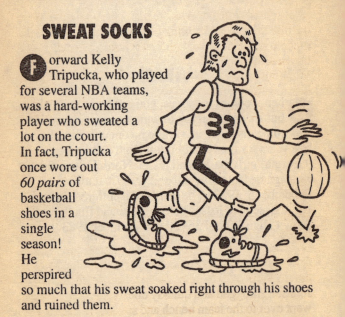

so much that his sweat soaked right through his shoes and ruined them.

WACKY RULE

How do you move a basketball up and down the court? You can pass the ball, but more often than not you dribble it. Dribbling is an important part of the modern game of basketball, but it wasn't always allowed. When basketball was invented by Dr. James Naismith in 1891, the only legal way to move the ball was to roll it or pass it. Dribbling was strictly forbidden. It wasn't until around 1900 that dribbling a basketball became a legal maneuver.

TAKE A SEAT

Gerald Johnson was a substitute player on the Oral Roberts University team in 1982. Johnson, who usually sat on the bench, was fooling around at practice taking half-court shots when assistant coach Mike O'Rourke walked into the gym. O'Rourke didn't think Johnson should waste time with long shots and told him to shoot only from game-situation positions. Johnson shrugged and quickly obeyed his coach. He went over to the team bench and sat down. He then picked up a ball and shot it toward the basket from a sitting position. Johnson may not have been a great player, but he had a great sense of humor!

POINT GUARDS?

Marion Boyd of Lonaconing Central High School in Maryland scored 156 points in one game on February 25, 1924. Marion's 156 points is a girls' national high school record. But if you think scoring over 100 points in a single girls' basketball game is rare, guess again. Over the years, at least 15 girls have scored over 100 points in a single game.

GAME GOOF

When the final buzzer sounded at the end of a basketball game between Lock Haven High School and Edinboro High School in Pennsylvania in 1981, everyone headed for the exits and locker rooms. Everyone believed Lock Haven had defeated Edinboro 84–82 and the game was over. But the game wasn't over. When the officials checked the official score books, they found that the game was really tied. The scorer had goofed and the scoreboard was wrong.

The solution to the problem was simple. The officials went into the locker rooms and had the players put their uniforms back on. The teams returned to the court and played an overtime period to determine the winner. The first overtime ended in another tie. Lock Haven finally won the game for good in the second overtime.

WASHED OUT

The University of Nevada at Las Vegas basketball team traveled to Oklahoma City, Oklahoma, for a game against Oklahoma City University on January 9, 1980. Unfortunately, the game had to be postponed because of *rain*. That's right! Rain in Oklahoma City was so heavy, it caused leaks in the roof of the State Fairgrounds Arena, where the game was to be played. The leaks were so bad that puddles formed on the basketball court below, washing away any hopes of playing the game.

FROM BAD TO WORSE

In 1980 the Mount Vernon College women's basketball team took on a squad from the University of the District of Columbia. It was a night the Mount Vernon team would like to forget. When the first half ended, Mount Vernon had scored a measly 4 points and was losing 63–4. It didn't seem as if things could get any worse, but they did. Mount Vernon scored only 7 more points in the second half, while the opposition scored 80 more points. The University of the District of Columbia ended up walloping Mount Vernon 143–11!

TEAM PROTEST

B owling Green State University was leading Ohio University 47–46 in a hotly contested Mid-American Conference game on January 20, 1984, when something strange happened. With seconds remaining in the contest, there was a mad scramble for the ball, and the official ruled the ball was last touched by an Ohio University player. When Coach Danny Nee of Ohio walked the length of the court to confront the official who made the controversial call, Nee was hit with a technical foul. David Jenkins of Bowling Green made the two foul shots to give Bowling Green a 49–46 lead. Then things got weird. There were four seconds left on the clock. Because of the technical, Bowling Green retained possession of the ball. But the Ohio players were so mad about the call on their coach, they just walked off the court in protest. With seconds remaining, the entire Ohio University team sat on the bench and watched as Bowling Green inbounded the ball uncontested and scored an easy basket to end the game 51–46.

SNEAKY SNEAKER

Momentum is a key factor in winning any sporting event. In February 1986, the Rutgers men's basketball team was building up momentum in a game against Temple University when a strange thing happened to cool off Rutgers' hot streak.

Rutgers had been down by 19 points to Temple at the half but was getting back into the game thanks to the dazzling play of the Knights' Darren Campbell. The Temple lead had been cut to only nine points when Campbell started to race downcourt. Suddenly, one of Campbell's sneakers came apart during play. The sole of the sneaker fell almost completely off.

Campbell started flopping around in his torn sneaker. Time had to be called and Campbell was taken out of the game. While he raced into the locker room to change his sneakers, play continued. Unfortunately, by the time he returned to the court ready to play again, Temple had stolen the momentum and surged ahead to a 15-point lead. Temple went on to win the game 71–53 because Rutgers lost momentum when its star player's sneaker flew apart.

FLAP!

FLAP!

FLAP!

RIGHT STATE, WRONG COLLEGE!

he Boston University Terriers were scheduled to take on Colgate University in a basketball game in December 1986. The Terriers, coached by Mike Jarvis, flew from Boston to Syracuse, New York, where a bus was waiting to transport the squad to Colgate's campus in Hamilton, New York. It was supposed to be a short trip, because Hamilton is only about 35 miles from Syracuse. But it didn't turn out that way.

Coach Jarvis and his team got on the bus, and off they went. The drive seemed to take a lot longer than expected. When the bus finally stopped outside a college gymnasium, Jarvis got off and couldn't believe his eyes. The bus driver had taken the BU team to Ithaca, New York, the home of Cornell University, which is about 75 miles from Hamilton! Boston University ended up at the wrong school! Coach Jarvis quickly called officials at Colgate, and when he explained the circumstances, the game was delayed. The bus turned around and drove to Hamilton, where it was supposed to go in the first place. All turned out well for Boston University in the end, as the Terriers beat Colgate 78–65.

NOT LETTER-PERFECT

igh school basketball coach Chet Gurick played varsity basketball for Brooklyn College in 1943 but didn't have a varsity letter to show for it. In 1944 Gurick was drafted into the army and never received the letter due him for his athletic accomplishments on the basketball court. In 1979, 36 years later, Brooklyn College finally awarded Chet Gurick his varsity letter in basketball.

FOOD FOR THOUGHT

Big Georgia Tech basketball player Dennis Scott lost 30 pounds during the 1990–91 season. When the new slim and trim Scott was introduced before a Georgia Tech game against Duke University that was played at Duke's stadium, the Duke fans greeted him in what they thought was a funny way. They tossed snack cakes and doughnuts at him from the stands. Duke coach Mike Krzyzewski quickly apologized for the not-so-sweet behavior of the Duke fans.

THAT'S A LOT OF JUMPING

Wilt Chamberlain, who played for several NBA teams from 1960 to 1973, did a lot of jumping on the court. Chamberlain pulled down a record 23,924 rebounds during his career. He was also a gentleman on the court. He played in 1,045 games— his entire NBA career—without ever fouling out.

WRONG-WAY SLAM

E verybody makes mistakes, but the mistake the Cleveland Cavaliers' Johnny Warren made in an NBA game against the Portland Trail Blazers in 1970 was a humdinger.

It was late in the game and the Cavaliers were down to the Blazers by three points. Cleveland coach Bill Fitch called a time-out. After a short pep talk by Fitch, the Cavaliers got the ball and seemed a bit disorganized and confused. Suddenly Cleveland guard Bobby Lewis saw Johnny Warren streaking down the court unguarded. Lewis fed Warren the ball, and Warren slammed it through the hoop for two points. Unfortunately, Warren had run the wrong way and jammed the ball into Portland's basket, scoring two points for the Trail Blazers! The mistake gave Portland a five-point lead, and they went on to win the game.

BUDDY BUDDY

When Seton Hall University met Duke University in the NCAA Basketball East Regional semifinals in 1992, it was a reunion of sorts for some of the players. Bobby Hurley, Duke's star point guard, had been a high school teammate of Seton Hall superstars Terry Dehere and Jerry Walker at St. Anthony's in New Jersey. What made the matchup even more strange for Hurley was that his brother, Danny Hurley, was a freshman player for the Seton Hall squad. Bobby Hurley took the family bragging rights from brother Danny as Duke defeated Seton Hall 81–69.

RIPPED APART

Jim Bain was a well-known college basketball official who was sometimes too zealous in signaling fouls. Early in his career, Bain was working a game at the University of Missouri when he raced across the baseline to signal a charging foul. Unfortunately, one of Bain's feet slid out from under him and he ended up doing a split just like a cheerleader. To add to his embarrassment, he ripped the seam of his trousers!

ENOUGH IS ENOUGH

Everyone reads about sports mismatches that pit powerful superteams against much weaker squads, with the result being a lopsided win for the favorite. But when powerful Essex County Community College took on tiny Englewood Cliffs College in January 1974, the final score was even more lopsided than expected. The two New Jersey junior colleges put on a show that became the worst defeat in junior college basketball history. Essex County Community College didn't just beat Englewood Cliffs—they pulverized them. The final score was 210–67, an astounding difference of 143 points.

LONG, LONG GAME!

Two teams of five players each from the Sigma Nu fraternity set a world record when they played a basketball game for 102 straight hours! The marathon court caper took place at Indiana University of Pennsylvania from April 13 through April 17, 1983.

CHAMP WHEREVER HE GOES

Coach Bill Sharman was a winner when it came to managing pro basketball teams. He won titles in three pro leagues and is the only coach to ever accomplish that feat. Sharman coached the Cleveland Pipers to the American Basketball League (ABL) championship in 1962. He then led the Utah Stars to the American Basketball Association (ABA) title in 1971 Finally, Sharman coached the Los Angeles Lakers to the National Basketball Association (NBA) championship in 1972. Once a winner, always a winner.

YOU AGAIN?

In 1980 Doug Moe and Billy Cunningham were both NBA coaches. Moe coached the San Antonio Spurs and Cunningham coached the Philadelphia 76ers. When the Spurs played the 76ers, the two coaches didn't meet for the first time. In fact, it was just the continuation of a long-term relationship between them. Moe and Cunningham attended Erasmus High School together in Brooklyn, New York, and later they both attended the University of North Carolina. It seems that where Moe and Cunningham were concerned, where one went the other followed.

TRIPLE TROUBLE

In 1957 the University of North Carolina posted a 32–0 season record and won the NCAA basketball tournament to take the national title. But putting the finishing touches on that perfect season wasn't easy. In the semifinals North Carolina had to beat a stubborn Michigan State team, and the game went into a triple overtime before North Carolina won it 74–70. Less than 24 hours later, North Carolina took on the University of Kansas in the NCAA finals and won 54–53 to capture the title. However, that game also went three overtime periods. So North Carolina won it all with two triple overtime wins in less than 24 hours in its final two games of the season.

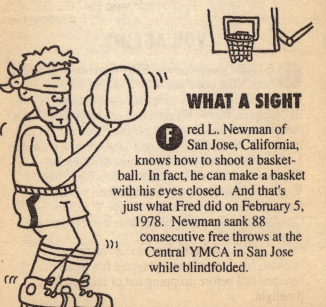

WHAT A SIGHT

Fred L. Newman of San Jose, California, knows how to shoot a basketball. In fact, he can make a basket with his eyes closed. And that's just what Fred did on February 5, 1978. Newman sank 88 consecutive free throws at the Central YMCA in San Jose while blindfolded.

POINT MAN

Center Clarence "Bevo" Francis was one of basketball's greatest scorers, although not many people today know his name. Bevo played at tiny Rio Grande College in southern Ohio. During the 1952–53 season, he poured in 116 points in a single game against Kentucky's Ashland Junior College (now Ashland Community College) as Rio Grande won 150–85. Bevo's point total was declared a record at first, but was then nullified because the points came against a two-year school that was not a bachelor's-degree-issuing institution.

Francis was upset, but he got his revenge in 1954. Against Hillsdale College, a small four-year school in Michigan, he scored *113* of his team's points in its 134–91 victory. Since this game was against an official four-year school, Francis' feat was declared a small-college record, which still stands today. But that wasn't the end of his basketball acomplishments.

After deciding to leave college, Bevo Francis signed to play with the Washington Generals, the team that tours with the Harlem Globetrotters. He later left the Generals and played a few years of semipro ball before dropping out of the basketball limelight.

TWO FOR YOU, TWO FOR US

High school basketball player Chris Kelly of Greybull High School in Wyoming pulled off one of the strangest four-point plays in basketball history during the 1965–66 season. Kelly was out on the floor when there was a mad scramble for a loose ball. He came up with the ball but lost his sense of direction. He pulled away from the pack and dribbled off toward the basket. Unfortunately, it was the other team's basket. Using perfect form, he went in for a lay-up and made the shot but was fouled in the act by the opposition.

Chris Kelly accidentally scored two points for the other team and then marched downcourt to the right basket to shoot two foul shots for his own team.

Kelly converted both foul shots, adding two points to his own team's score. So in a bizarre sequence of events, Chris Kelly scored two points for his opponents and two points for his own team on the very same play'

DEFENSIVE STRUGGLE

The Fort Mill High School girls' basketball team squared off against Clover High School's squad in one of the strangest defensive battles in basketball history. The game, which took place in February 1980 in South Carolina, started slow, to say the least. At the end of the first half, Clover led by the low, low score of 2–0! Things didn't get much more productive in the second half. Clover scored four more points while Fort Mill High managed to sink only one basket late in the contest. When the final buzzer sounded, Clover beat Fort Mill by the crazy score of 6–2!

RUNNING GAME

Basketball is a strenuous game—you have to be able to run a great distance. To prove that point, Coach Ben Peck of Middlebury College, in Vermont, once strapped pedometers, which measure how far a person runs or walks, to the feet of his players before a game. At the end of the game, Peck discovered that his team had covered almost 25 miles. Both of the guards, who seldom run all the way up and down the length of the court, had run just over 2½ miles each while the team's center had traveled a distance of just over four miles. The forwards had run over five miles each!

HOW MANY SHOTS?

Basketball official Jimmy Enright almost made a whopper of an error in a game he officiated between Purdue University and the University of Minnesota. The game was a hard-fought contest played on Purdue's home court. When Minnesota's Eddie Kalafat was fouled in the act of shooting, Enright blew his whistle and awarded Kalafat two shots.

Kalafat sank the first of his two shots. Then Purdue called a time-out. When the players returned to the court for the second shot, Enright handed Kalafat the ball and held up *two fingers*, indicating that Kalafat still had two shots.

Quickly, Ray Eddy, the Purdue coach, ran up to the official and screamed, "Jim, he shot one already!"

Enright looked at Eddy and asked, "Scout's honor, Ray?"

"Yup," answered the Purdue coach.

Enright's memory returned, and he let Kalafat take the one remaining shot due him.

GREAT, BUT...

High school star Rick Morrill had a terrific basketball game against Alvirne High School in New Hampshire in 1965. He scored 78 points, but unfortunately he didn't get to enjoy his accomplishment. Morrill's Pembroke Academy team lost to Alvirne 111–96 in that contest. Rick Morrill scored the most points ever in a losing cause for a high school team.

DON'T KNOCK YOURSELF OUT

John Stobel of North Andover High School, in Massachusetts, was the kind of player who would knock himself out trying to win a game. In fact, in a game against Wareham High School, that's just what he did. After taking a long pass from a teammate, Stobel jumped up and shot the ball. Unfortunately, he came crashing down to the floor, hit his head, and knocked himself out. When Stobel regained consciousness ten minutes later, he found out he'd scored the game-winning points on his knock-out shot. Luckily, he was not seriously injured.

KNIGHT TIME

When it comes to basketball, Bobby Knight was and still is a winner. In 1960 Knight was a player on the Ohio State team that won the NCAA basketball championship. In 1976 he returned to the NCAA tourney as a coach and watched his Indiana University team take the crown. Bobby Knight was the first person to win college basketball titles as a player and as a coach.

GAME TIME ALREADY?

The Temple University Owls and the West Virginia University Mountaineers were locked in an intense Atlantic-10 basketball contest on January 11, 1990. The teams were tied for first place in the conference and tied in the game at 66, with a little over three minutes left to play. Temple had the ball and called a time-out. The players from both teams huddled with their respective coaches in front of their benches to plot strategy.

At the end of the time-out period, a horn sounded signaling the teams to get ready to play. According to the rules, a team has 15 seconds to return to the court after a time-out. Temple broke from Coach John Chaney's huddle and took their place on the court. The Mountaineers remained in their huddle talking with their coach, Gale Catlett. When the next horn sounded, signaling the end of the 15-second grace period, West Virginia was still huddled and not on the court ready to play.

So what did the officials do? They handed the ball to the Temple players and started the game without the Mountaineers on the court. Temple inbounded the ball and scored an easy lay-up as the befuddled Mountaineers frantically rushed back out on the court. The Owls went on to win 73–69.

REMEMBER THIS!

Muhlenberg College and Lehigh University are intense rivals when it comes to basketball. During the 1966–67 season, Lehigh earned a victory in the first seasonal meeting between the two schools, which are both located in eastern Pennsylvania. Lehigh won that game by a 13-point margin.

Ken Moyer, the head basketball coach at Muhlenberg, was so disappointed over the loss that he prepared his team for the next meeting of the schools in a unique way. He taped the word "Remember" to his players' jerseys for the contest. Apparently the tactic backfired. The Muhlenberg players remembered their first game against Lehigh all too well. They lost the second game against Lehigh by the same 13-point margin!

SHORT TRIP

Modern college basketball teams usually have to travel all around the country to play in various tournaments. But in 1958 the University of Kentucky didn't have to go far to be crowned the best basketball team in the country. That year, Kentucky won the Mideast Regional playoff game, which was played in its home city of Lexington, Kentucky, to advance to the Final Four. Kentucky then played in the championship round, which was held in Louisville, Kentucky, and beat Seattle University 84–72 to take the national title. Kentucky won the 1958 NCAA tourney without ever having to leave its home state!

TALLY-WHOA!

Can you imagine scoring 184 points in a pro basketball contest and *losing* the game? That's what happened to the Denver Nuggets on December 13, 1983. At the end of regulation time, their game against the Detroit Pistons was tied 145–145. After three overtime periods, Detroit finally prevailed 186–184. The combined score of 370 points is still an NBA record.

The combined scoring record in a game ending in *regulation* time is 318 points, set when the Denver Nuggets defeated the San Antonio Spurs 163–155 on January 11, 1984.

FRIENDLY FOUL

Everybody makes a mistake once in a while, and basketball officials are no exception. In March 1932, referee Frank Lane made one big goof in a game he was officiating between the University of Kentucky and Vanderbilt University.

During some heated play under the Kentucky backboard, Lane whistled a foul against Dutch Kreuter for hitting Kentucky's Aggie Sale across the arms while Sale was in the act of shooting. Sale went to the foul line to shoot two, but before he could, a Vanderbilt player approached Lane and asked the official to point out the person guilty of the foul. Lane pointed out Dutch Kreuter and then realized his goof. Kreuter and Sales were both members of the Kentucky Wildcats! A player can't be guilty of fouling his own teammate. The official had made a huge mistake. However, rather than admit he'd messed up, Frank Lane counted the foul against Kreuter and instead gave a *Vanderbilt* player the free throws. Vanderbilt made both points and eventually won the game marred by that strange call, 32–31!

CAREER CUT SHORT

Angelo "Hank" Luisetti is generally credited with being the basketball player who popularized the one-handed shot. Prior to the success Luisetti had with his one-handed shot, most basketball stars in the 1930's shot the ball with two hands. Luisetti, who was a great high school player in San Francisco, California, went on to college basketball glory at Stanford University. Using his one-handed shot, he once poured in 50 points in a single game against a strong Duquesne team.

Hank Luisetti became well known all over the country and even starred in a Hollywood movie. He probably would have been a great pro except that he came down with spinal meningitis after only three years of playing college ball. Hank fought the disease bravely and won the battle for his life, but his basketball career was abruptly ended. So the man who invented the one-handed shot every pro uses today never got a chance to shoot the ball his way in a professional game.

LUCKY SEVEN

In the early days of basketball, many of the rules were nothing like the rules that govern the modern game. For example, when Yale University played Wesleyan University in the very first inter-collegiate basketball game, which was held on December 10, 1896, in New Haven, Connecticut, there was something very different about the contest. The teams played with *seven* players each on the court at one time instead of the five players we use today. Yale won that game.

When teams finally started using five players on each side, Yale was involved again. In 1897 the first intercollegiate basketball game with five players on a side was played between Yale and the University of Pennsylvania. Yale won that one, too.

CHRISTMAS PRESENT

Two girls' high school teams got their Christmas presents early in December 1991. First, Blair High School of Pasadena, California, beat Marshall Fundamental High of Pasadena 62–0 in a game played on December 4, 1991.

Following Blair High's example, Pitkin High School's girls' basketball team improved on that stat a bit. The team from southwest Louisiana beat home-state rival Forest Hill High 80–0 on December 14, 1991.

NO JOKE

Coach Jerry Reynolds of the Sacramento Kings had quite a reputation for pulling jokes and pranks. So when Reynolds collapsed to the floor during a home game against the Portland Trail Blazers, everyone thought he was just fooling around. The referee even called a technical foul against Reynolds because he thought the coach was mocking his calls. It took a while for fans, players, officials, and everyone else in the building to realize that Coach Reynolds *wasn't* kidding around. He had hyper-ventilated and actually passed out in front of the Kings' bench!

When everyone realized that Reynolds wasn't faking his condition, help was quickly summoned. The coach eventually came to and was rushed to a nearby hospital. Luckily tests proved negative. But through the entire ordeal, Jerry Reynolds never lost his keen sense of humor. One of the first things he asked for when they wheeled him into the emergency room was a bag of popcorn!

LIKE FATHER, LIKE...DAUGHTER?

When John Somogyi played basketball for Saint Peter's High School in New Brunswick, New Jersey, in the late 1960's, he was regarded as one of the best scoring guards in the country. In fact, John went on to set a New Jersey scoring record for high school players in 1967. Somogyi's career total of 3,310 points erased basketball broadcaster Bill Raftery's name from the New Jersey record books (2,120 career points) and established a New Jersey high school career scoring mark that stood for 24 seasons.

Being a good sport, John wasn't too upset when his state mark for career points was eclipsed in February 1992. After all, the person who established the new record did attend Saint Peter's High School in New Brunswick, John's alma mater. In addition, the new record holder had several other things in common with the previous record holder. The player who broke the record wore uniform number 24, which was John's old number. Strangest of all was the fact that the new record holder was named Kristen Somogyi! In 1992, John Somogyi's daughter, Kristen, broke her father's 24-year-old high school career scoring mark. She set a new standard for the most points scored by a high school player in New Jersey — boy or girl — by chalking up 3,988 points in her career.

POINTLESS PROS

An NBA game is supposed to be jam-packed with action, thrills, and lots of scoring. But that wasn't the case on November 22, 1950, when the Fort Wayne Pistons traveled to Minneapolis for a game against the NBA champion Minneapolis Lakers, who were led by George Mikan. Mikan, who was 6'10", was the most dominant player in the NBA at the time and a great scorer.

The Pistons figured the only way they could defeat the Lakers was to slow down the pace of the game to keep Mikan from scoring. And slow it down they did. At the end of the first period of play, Fort Wayne led 8–7. At the half, the lead changed hands and Minneapolis led 13–11.

The second half was just as boring as the first. The Pistons kept holding the ball. The third period ended with the Lakers leading 17–16. The final period practically put the fans to sleep. The Lakers added one point to make their game total 18, while the Pistons added 3 to up their total to 19. Fort Wayne got the win in one of the most boring basketball games in NBA history. George Mikan didn't score a lot of points, but he tallied 15 of the Lakers' 18 points.

Fans, sportswriters, and league officials were so angered by the boring game that they churned up a storm of protest. League president Maurice Podoloff agreed that games like the Pistons' 19–18 win had no place in the NBA. He saw to it that a 24-second clock was added to the rule book. The rule meant that teams could no longer hold the ball and stall. They had only 24 seconds to handle the ball before taking at least one shot, or possession of the ball would go to the other team.

SWAPPING PLAYERS

It's a common thing for two National Basketball Association teams to swap baskets in a game. But is it possible for two teams to swap players in a game? Amazingly, that's what happened during the 1978–79 season in a game between the New Jersey Nets and the Philadelphia 76ers.

In a game early in the season, Al Skinner and Eric Money played for the Nets, and Harvey Catchings played for Philadelphia. The game was suspended because of a protest and was scheduled to be made up at a later date. Before the game could be replayed, however, the Nets traded Skinner and Money to the 76ers in exchange for Catchings and another player who was injured when the teams first met.

When the suspended game was finally continued, Eric Money and Al Skinner played for Philadelphia against Harvey Catchings and his New Jersey Nets teammates. Thus, those three players played for both teams in the same game. It's wacky, but true.

CLOSE BUT NO RECORD

When Morningside High School took on South Torrance High School in a California girls' high school basketball game in 1990, the result was almost a national single-game scoring record for Morningside's Lisa Leslie. Leslie scored 49 points in the first quarter and 52 points in the second quarter to help give Morningside a lopsided 102–24 lead over South Torrance at halftime. Since the modern high school scoring record for girls in a single game was 105 points, Leslie was certain that she'd set a new record before the game was over.

Unfortunately, the South Torrance High squad decided to call the game quits after the first half. They refused to take the floor when the second half began, and their coach supported their decision. The reason South Torrance refused to continue was that they had begun the game with only six players. When two fouled out before the second half ended, the team had only four players to finish the game.

Since South Torrance refused to take the court with four players, officials charged South Torrance with delay-of-game penalties and allowed Lisa Leslie to shoot four foul shots in an attempt to equal the record. She made all four and tied the mark. Afterward, when the league commissioner reviewed the game, he took away Leslie's points and ruled the game officially over at the half. It was a great game for Lisa Leslie, even though she didn't equal the record.

BIG WINNER

There have been a lot of great winning high school teams. However, no basketball team has ever been more successful than the girls' team at Baskins High School in Louisiana during the late 1940's and early 1950's. Under Coach Edna Tarbutton, Baskins won a national record 218 consecutive games from 1947 to 1953, a winning streak that may never be broken. During Tarbutton's first nine seasons at Baskins, she won an astounding 343 games and lost only 12. Her team also won eight state championships during that time. No other girls' high school basketball coach in history has ever been as successful as Edna Tarbutton.

BIG MONEY

Nat Holman won lasting fame in basketball as the coach of City College in New York. CCNY is the only school in history to win both the NCAA tourney and the NIT in the same year (1950), and it was Holman who coached that squad.

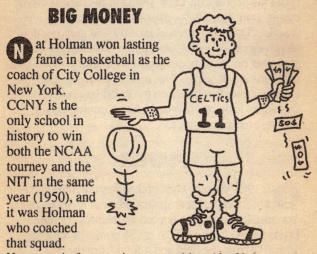

However, before turning to coaching, Nat Holman was a star pro player for the original, pre-NBA Boston Celtics. But Holman never made big bucks as a pro. He was paid a mere six dollars a game to play for Boston.

ENJOY YOUR TRIP?

Darryl Dawkins was a young NBA player who liked to joke around and have fun when he played for the Philadelphia 76ers in 1978. Dawkins was fooling around at practice one day when Coach Billy Cunningham decided to put an end to Dawkins' antics. He took Dawkins off the court and yelled at him about taking things more seriously—especially basketball practice. Dawkins listened silently and then nodded in agreement. Coach Cunningham was certain he'd made his point, so he turned to walk away. As he did, Dawkins stuck out his foot and playfully tripped Cunningham. Everyone on the court laughed at Dawkins' little prank—including Cunningham. It was just too funny not to.

PERFECT

In 1983 Walter Davis of the Phoenix Suns had a hot shooting hand against the Seattle Supersonics. You might even say he burned up the backboards. Davis scored the first 34 of his 36 points by shooting 15 for 15 from the field and 4 for 4 from the line. His 34 straight points without a miss broke a 22-year-old NBA record formerly held by Larry Costello (32 points without a miss).

COAT CAPER

Being a college, pro, or high school coach isn't an easy job. Coaches have been known to lose their tempers and do irrational things. The pressure once got to Coach Ray Eddy of Purdue during a hard-fought home game. Eddy got so upset that he tore off the sports jacket he was wearing, balled it up in his hands, and hurled it into the stands.

As soon as he came to his senses, Eddy yelled for a time-out. He dashed into the stands to hunt for the coat he'd angrily thrown away. In his fit of temper, Eddy had forgotten that his team was leaving for a two-day road trip right after the game, and that all of his team's meal money was in a pocket of his coat! Luckily for the coach and the Purdue team, Eddy managed to recover his jacket and the money.

SON OF A GUN

S ometimes coaches go to extremes to make an official listen to their pleas. A case in point is how Coach Joe Cipriano of the University of Nebraska got the attention of official Jim Bain during a game against the University of Oklahoma.

During the game, two players ended up running into the stands on a fast break. Bain blew his whistle so the players could get out of the stands. Meanwhile, the Oklahoma trainer came over to make sure no players had been hurt. Cipriano ran up to Bain at the scorer's table to demand that Oklahoma be charged with a time-out. In the confusion, however, Cipriano couldn't get Bain's attention. In desperation, Cipriano grabbed the blank gun used by the game's timer (in the early days of basketball, a gun was fired to signal the end of play because there was no buzzer) and fired it. The noise was so loud, it scared not only the official but Coach Cipriano, who quickly put the gun down and raced back to his seat. John MacLeod, the Oklahoma coach, wanted a technical foul called against Nebraska because Cipriano had fired the timer's gun. But Bain decided not to penalize the Nebraska team or charge the Oklahoma team with a time-out, and play continued.

PHEW!
70-MINUTE MAN

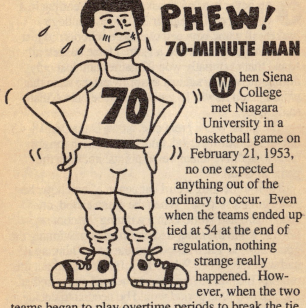

When Siena College met Niagara University in a basketball game on February 21, 1953, no one expected anything out of the ordinary to occur. Even when the teams ended up tied at 54 at the end of regulation, nothing strange really happened. However, when the two teams began to play overtime periods to break the tie, the game got a little wacky. At the end of the first overtime, the game was tied again — 61–61. When the second overtime expired, the score was 63–63. It was 65–65 when the third overtime ended. After the fourth overtime, the teams were deadlocked 72–72. When the fifth overtime concluded, it was Siena 77, Niagara 77. Finally, in the sixth overtime, Niagara won the game 88–81. The marathon basketball game lasted a rare six overtime periods and consisted of 70 minutes of playing time! Eddie Fleming of Niagara played all 70 minutes of the game and was one tired player at the end of the contest. To commemorate his feat of endurance that day, his uniform number was later changed to — what else...70!

NO OVERTIME

You never hear of a basketball game ending in a tie. But on December 31, 1935, a college basketball game between two large schools did just that. The game matched a Notre Dame basketball squad that eventually won 22 games and lost only 2 during the season against a Northwestern team that would go on to win 13 games and lose only 6 that same year.

The game was a great one. Notre Dame led 18–13 late in the fourth period, but Northwestern fought back to add five unanswered points, knotting the game at 18 all.

Then something weird happened. Somehow the score got messed up. When the game ended, one scoreboard had Notre Dame winning the contest 20–19, while the other had Northwestern winning the game 20–19. Each school left the court thinking it had won the game. When the officials sorted out the mix-up, they discovered the game was really tied at 20. An overtime period would be needed to decide a winner. The problem was that the teams had already changed and were ready to leave. Both schools decided it was best to just call the game between them a tie, and that's exactly what they did!

CLOSING STORY

Good things don't always come to a good end. In February 1980, the Syracuse Orangemen played their last game ever at their old home court in Manley Field House. The Orangemen would be moving into Syracuse's new Carrier Dome the following year.

Manley Field House had been a great place to play for Syracuse. Going into that final game, the Orangemen had won 57 consecutive home games. In fact, Coach Jim Boeheim had never lost a game at Manley since he had been named the head man at Syracuse. Naturally, the Orangemen and their coach wanted to exit the old arena as winners, with their consecutive home-game winning streak intact.

Unfortunately, the visiting Georgetown Hoyas had something different in mind. Underdog Georgetown made the Orangemen's last game at Manley a nightmare rather than a treasured memory. Favored Syracuse lost its final game at Manley, and Coach Jim Boeheim lost his only game at Manley Field House as Georgetown won the contest 52–50!

INDEX